# MINECRAFTER

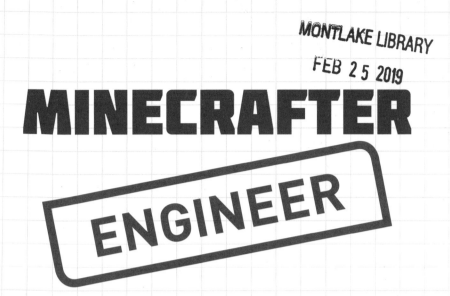

## ENGINEER

# AWESOME MOB GRINDERS
# AND FARMS

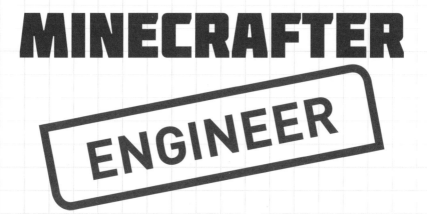

# MINECRAFTER ENGINEER

## AWESOME MOB GRINDERS AND FARMS

**Contraptions for Getting the Loot**

## MEGAN MILLER

Sky Pony Press
New York

Sky Pony Press books may be purchased in bulk at special discounts for sales promotion, corporate gifts, fund-raising, or educational purposes. Special editions can also be created to specifications. For details, contact the Special Sales Department, Sky Pony Press, 307 West 36th Street, 11th Floor, New York, NY 10018 or info@skyhorsepublishing.com.

Sky Pony® is a registered trademark of Skyhorse Publishing, Inc.®, a Delaware corporation.

Minecraft® is a registered trademark of Notch Development AB. The Minecraft game is copyright © Mojang AB.

Visit our website at www.skyponypress.com.

Authors, books, and more at SkyPonyPressBlog.com.

10 9 8 7 6 5 4 3 2 1

Cover and interior art by Megan Miller

Cover design by Michael Short
Book design by Megan Miller

Print ISBN: 978-1-5107-3765-5

Printed in China

# CONTENTS

# INTRODUCTION

**SOMETIMES IN MINECRAFT YOU NEED STUFF.** Lots of stuff. Lots of zombie flesh to trade with villagers, lots of villagers to trade with, or lots of XP to make the most OP enchanted sword. Now you can engineer a solution! The mob farms in this book will help you get the loot, from gun powder to blaze rods. Some of the farms use redstone but are not terribly difficult, so you should be able to complete each farm on your path to world domination!

The farms in this book work for the 1.12.2 version of Minecraft Java Edition. Several are adapted from farms created or modified by expert redstoners and Minecrafters such as Etho, Tango Tek, Avomance, and impulseSV, who are also some of my favorite YouTubers! If you like to learn while watching videos, I recommend them.

Along with step-by-step screens from Minecraft, this guide also includes technical drawings and diagrams to help show where blocks go. Engineers use technical drawings, schematics, and blueprints to specify exactly where mechanisms are placed and how they are built.

Don't forget to share your own Minecraft engineering accomplishments with me online. If you build any of these farms or other custom engineering designs, I'd love to see them! You, or a family member, can tweet me at @meganfmiller to showcase your work.

# Protect Your Builds

PROTECT ANY BUILDS YOU MAKE THAT INCLUDE REDSTONE, BECAUSE MOST REDSTONE ELEMENTS (SUCH AS REPEATERS, REDSTONE DUST, AND MORE) WILL BREAK AND FLOAT AWAY WHEN THEY ARE TOUCHED BY FLOWING WATER. AN ACCIDENTAL PLACEMENT OF WATER CAN WIPE OUT YOUR BUILD. WHEN YOU DO BUILD A CONTAINING STRUCTURE FOR YOUR FARMS TO PROTECT REDSTONE, MAKE SURE TO LEAVE SPACE BETWEEN YOUR REDSTONE ELEMENTS AND THE STRUCTURE. THIS STEP HELPS PREVENT PLACING BLOCKS THAT COULD INTERFERE WITH A REDSTONE SIGNAL. THE EXTRA SPACE WILL ALSO ALLOW YOU TO MOVE AROUND THE BUILD IF YOU NEED TO CHECK OR FIX SOMETHING LATER.

ALSO, REMEMBER TO LIGHT UP YOUR BUILDS AS YOU GO. A CREEPER IS JUST AS INTERESTED IN BLOWING UP REDSTONE AS IT IS IN DEMOLISHING YOUR BASE.

# CHAPTER 1
# ALL-PURPOSE, NO-REDSTONE MOB FARM

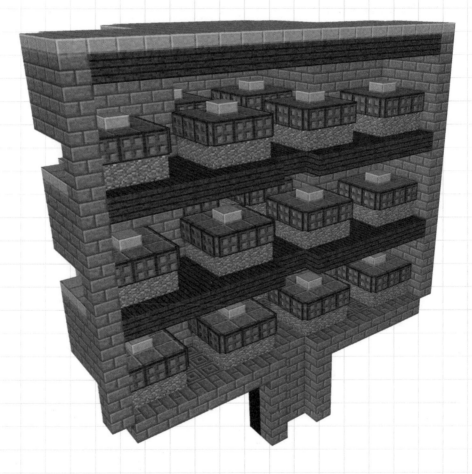

**YOU CAN MAKE THIS CLASSIC MOB-GRINDING** farm soon after you start your world. You'll just need plenty of cobble, wood, and enough iron for a couple of buckets and four hoppers. It's not a pretty farm, but it will get you bones, zombie flesh, gunpowder, arrows, and other loot from skeletons, zombies, and creepers.

# Planning Mob Grinders

This farm takes advantage of several key features of mobs and mob spawning rules.

- Hostile mobs treat open trapdoors as if they are solid blocks to walk on.

- Hostile mobs can be easily pushed by water flows.

- Overworld hostile mobs spawn at light level 7 and below.

- Hostile mobs spawn 24 blocks to 240 blocks away from a player but despawn instantly if they are more than 128 blocks away from a player. This means the mob-spawning area around a player is a doughnut shape from 24 to 128 blocks away. In addition, mobs despawn gradually if they are farther than 32 blocks away from a player.

- Fall damage is 1 heart of damage for each block fallen after 3 blocks. That means a fall of 23 blocks causes 20 hearts of damage, and will kill skeletons, zombies, and creepers.

- The mob cap is the maximum number of mobs allowed in a world. In a single-player world, the default mob cap for hostile mobs is 70. That means it is very important when you build a mob farm that doesn't use a spawner to ensure mobs are spawning only in your farm, and not in nearby caves or forests. Around any mob farm that is limited by the mob cap, you will want to prevent other spawns within a radius of 128 blocks from where you, the player, are located.

This mob farm is made efficient by placing it about 150 blocks above ground. It places the location you stand in to activate spawning too far away from any other surfaces that mobs could spawn in, so they'll only be spawning in your farm. If you place the farm over a Deep Ocean biome, in which the water is at least 20 blocks deep, you can build it 20 blocks closer to water level.

We'll build this farm on land. If you are building over Deep Ocean, make the funnel leading up to the spawning platforms 20 blocks shorter. To build on ocean, use a lily pad directly on the water surface. Then you can place your first block above the lily pad.

# Be a Smart Engineer

AS WITH ALL OF THE BUILDS IN THIS BOOK, THE STEP BY STEP INSTRUCTIONS ARE FOR THE FINAL STRUCTURE, AND DON'T INCLUDE TIPS FOR SECURING AREAS, LIGHTING ROOFS, AND OTHER SURFACES TO PREVENT SPAWNING OUTSIDE THE FARM, OR PLACING TEMPORARY LADDERS OR STAIRS THAT ASSIST THE BUILDER IN SURVIVAL MODE.

## Step by Step

1.  Build any type of a pillar 127 blocks tall, along with ladders to climb up. I am using several different types of block, but you can use cobblestone for this entire farm.

2.  At the top of the pillar, build a platform 8 blocks long and 4 wide, extending away from the pillar. This is the platform that you will stand on when activating the farm above.

# All-Purpose, No-Redstone Farm

## SPAWNING LAYER FLOORPLAN

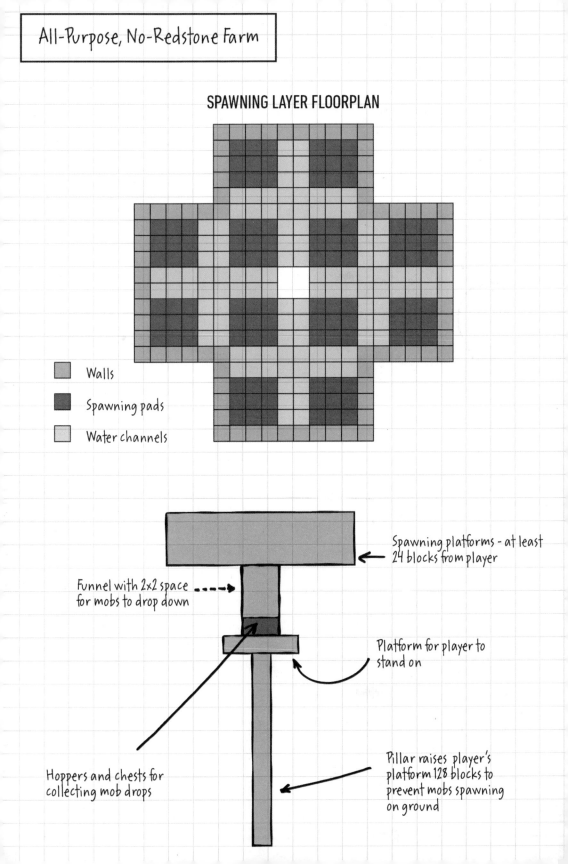

Walls

Spawning pads

Water channels

Spawning platforms - at least 24 blocks from player

Funnel with 2x2 space for mobs to drop down

Platform for player to stand on

Hoppers and chests for collecting mob drops

Pillar raises player's platform 128 blocks to prevent mobs spawning on ground

**3.** At the end of the platform is where we'll put the funnel or tower that mobs drop down. I've outlined where the walls go with temporary yellow wool blocks.

**4.** Place a double chest to store drops, as shown.

# XP Anyone?

IF YOU WANT TO MODIFY THIS BUILD INTO AN XP FARM, MAKE THE FUNNEL 3 BLOCKS SHORTER AND OPEN UP SPACE TO HIT THE MOBS THROUGH AT THE BOTTOM PLATFORM. PLACE CARPET OVER THE HOPPER TO HELP XP TO FLOW TO YOU. PLACE CARPET OVER THE BOTTOM OF ANY FULL BLOCK SPACES TO PREVENT BABY ZOMBIES FROM GETTING OUT. ALSO, IF YOU HAVE MORE THAN 1 SPAWNING LAYER, PLACE 4 VINES INSIDE THE FUNNEL AT THE BOTTOM LAYER OF THE FARM. THE VINES MOMENTARILY SLOW THE FALLING MOBS AND SET THEIR FALL DISTANCES (AND DAMAGE) TO JUST THE LENGTH OF THE FUNNEL MINUS 1 BLOCK. MOST MOBS THAT FALL NOW SHOULD BE KILLABLE WITH 1, SOMETIMES 2 HITS, DEPENDING ON WHETHER THEY SPAWN WITH ARMOR OR ARE THE WITCHES, WHO HAVE HIGHER HEALTH.

**5.** Behind the chest, place 4 hoppers pointing toward the chest.

**6.** Around the chest and hoppers, build the first layer of the funnel's walls, as shown.

7. Build the second and third layer of the funnels walls, using at least 2 glass blocks above the chest. Glass blocks will let you see the mobs in their final moments of crashing down; also, a chest can still open with glass blocks right above it.

8. We want the funnel to be 24 blocks tall (not including the floor of the platform we are building in the next step), so build another 21 levels to the funnel.

**9.** At the top of the funnel, build out 4 arms that are 8 blocks long total and 2 blocks wide, as shown, leaving clear the center of the funnel where mobs will drop.

**10.** Build 16 3x3 squares at the beginning and ending of the arms, as shown. These show where the mob spawning pads will go.

**11.** Finish building out the bottom of the farm by filling in the 3x2 gaps between the spawning pad areas. (I've used chiseled stone here.)

**12.** Build each of the 12 spawning pad areas to be 2 blocks high.

**13.** Build walls around this entire platform that are 3 blocks higher than the spawning pads (5 blocks taller than the floor between the pads).

**14.** If you want to prevent spiders from spawning, place a slab in the middle of each spawning pad. (Spiders can occasionally clog the funnel.)

**15.** At the end of one of the arms built in Step 9, place 2 buckets of water against the 2 blocks of the back wall. The water will flow directly to the central funnel without flowing into the funnel.

**16.** Do the same for the other 3 arms. These are the main channels of water pushing the mobs.

**17.** Along one of the main channels, at the front of the right back spawn pad, place a single bucket of water at the outer wall.

**18.** Do the same on the pad that is across the main channel. These two side channels now flow into the main channel.

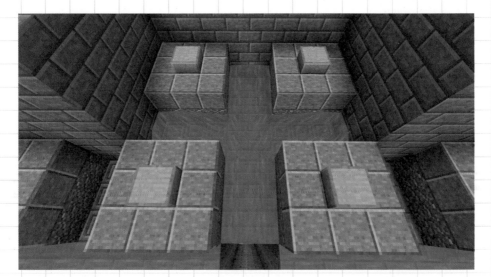

**19.** Now repeat Steps 17 and 18 for the other 3 main channels of the farm.

**20.** To make the mobs think they are walking onto solid blocks instead of into the water channels, place wooden trapdoors along each exposed edge of the 16 spawn pads.

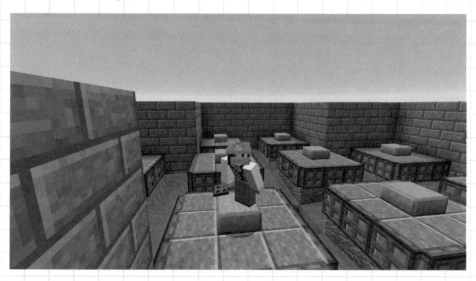

**21.** Now fill in between the tops of the walls to make the spawning platform ceiling. You've completed 1 layer of the mob farm. If you want to stop here, slab over the ceiling to prevent mobs spawning on it.

**22.** If you want to reap even more loot, add 1 or more additional layers, using the ceiling as the floor of the next layer. Don't forget to break open a hole into the main funnel!

**23.** When you are done adding layers, fill in the ceiling as you did in Step 21 and then slab over this. It's time to loiter around the bottom platform and chest and start collecting your rewards. Note: Sometimes witches will spawn. As they have higher HP than the other mobs, they'll survive the drop and be able to regenerate health. You may want to add a way to kill these witches off. For example, a trapdoor opening into the funnel through which you can shoot arrows.

# CHAPTER 2
# VILLAGER BREEDER

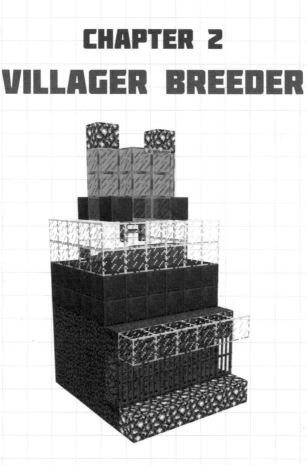

**BUILDING A VILLAGER BREEDER IS A WAY** to get the best trades: trades for emeralds, and emeralds for the most powerful enchanted books and weapons. The goal is to breed villagers and take just those villagers with the trades you want to a safe location where it is easy for you to trade with them. This tutorial doesn't cover what to do with any villagers you don't want. I'll suggest transporting them back to another village to live their days out happily!

This simple villager breeder will produce a villager about every 10 minutes. It is based on a few village mechanics, including villager willingness to breed, the size of the village, and how villagers locate their village and count villagers.

## Step by Step

1. Build a 6 block long x 5 block wide rectangle of building blocks with 2 missing blocks in the front, as shown. This will be the base of the farm.

2. Add a second layer of blocks above this.

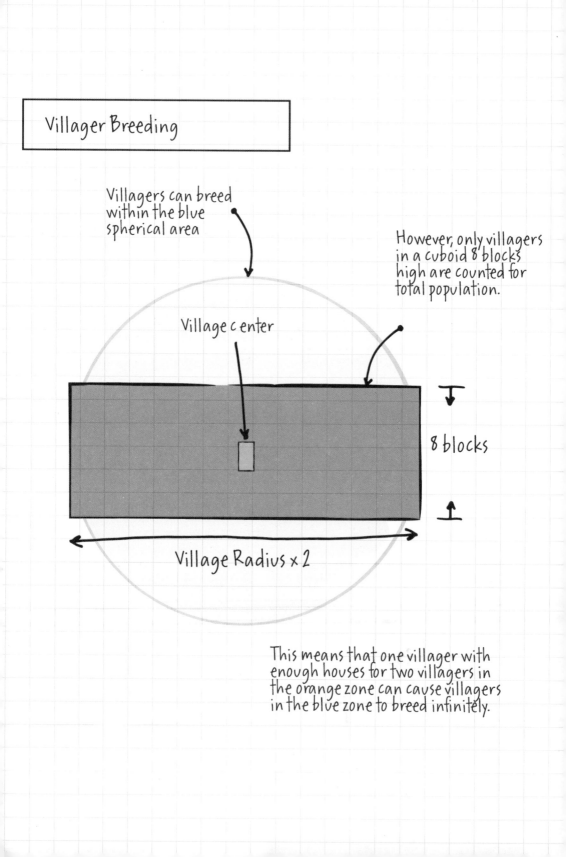

Villager Breeding

Villagers can breed within the blue spherical area

However, only villagers in a cuboid 8 blocks high are counted for total population.

Village center

8 blocks

Village Radius x 2

This means that one villager with enough houses for two villagers in the orange zone can cause villagers in the blue zone to breed infinitely.

**3.** Add a row of glass blocks above and around the sides the base, as if the missing blocks weren't missing.

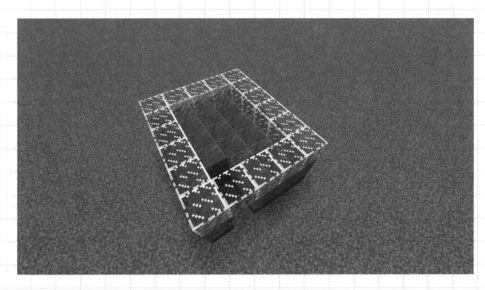

**4.** Add a second row of glass blocks above this.

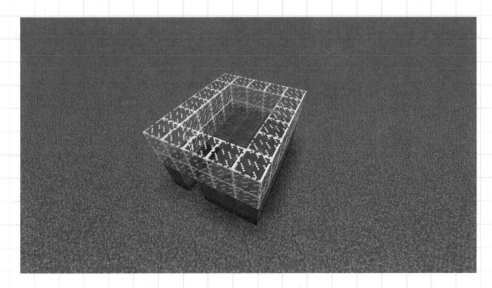

**5.** In the center of the enclosure, place 2 temporary blocks as shown.

**6.** On top of each of the 2 temporary blocks, place a fence. The villagers who will breed will stand on these.

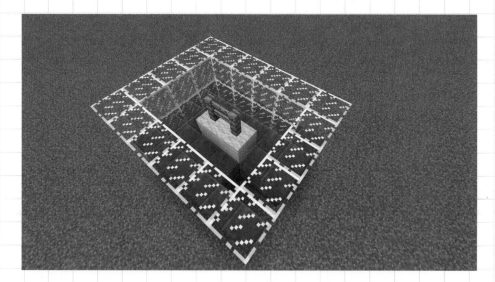

**7.** Above each of the 2 fence posts, place 2 more temporary blocks, as shown. These placeholding blocks show where the villagers will go.

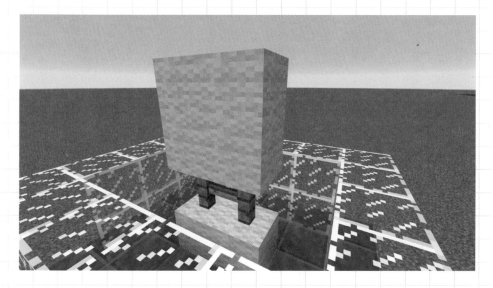

**8.** Place a row of 6 glass blocks around the bottom of the villager placeholding blocks.

**9.** Place another row above these.

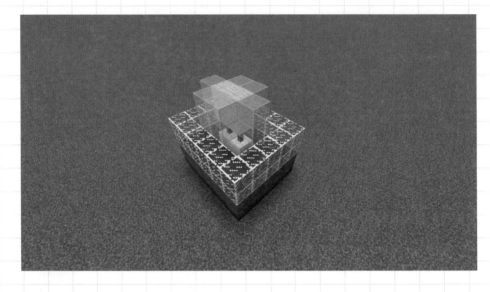

**10.** Knock out the temporary blocks and add 1 more row of glass blocks to the villager enclosure.

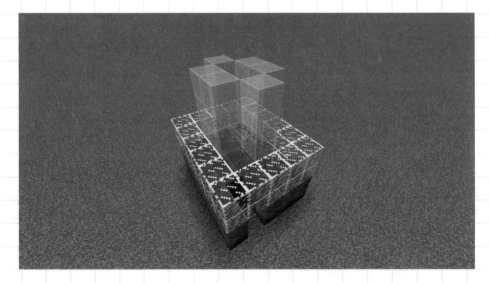

**11.** On one side of the structure, dig a hole that is 6 blocks long and 3 deep, as shown. This is where the "village" will be placed.

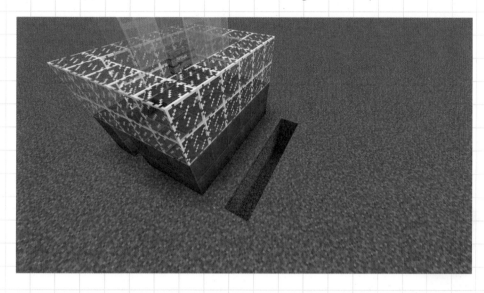

**12.** At the bottom of this shaft, dig out a space beneath the farm that is 6 blocks long, 2 high, and 1 deep, as shown.

**13.** Place 6 doors to enclose the dugout you made in Step 12.

**14.** It is time to bring the villagers in. You can do this however you like. One way is to push the villagers into minecarts. Then you can transport them by rail to a temporary platform above the enclosure and push them in.

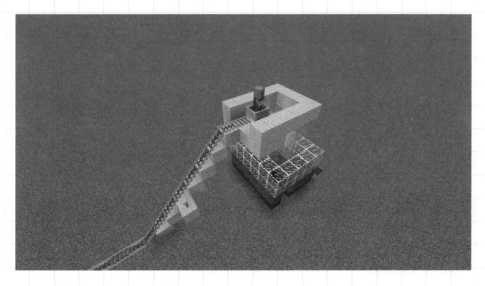

**15.** Right now, if you throw carrots to the villagers, the carrots will drop through the fences. To prevent this, we push glass blocks into the bottom halves of the villagers using pistons. The villagers won't take any damage from this. First, on one side of the enclosure, place 2 glass blocks, as shown.

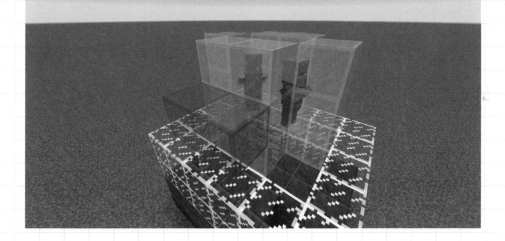

**16.** Use temporary blocks to place pistons (not sticky pistons) facing into the 2 glass blocks.

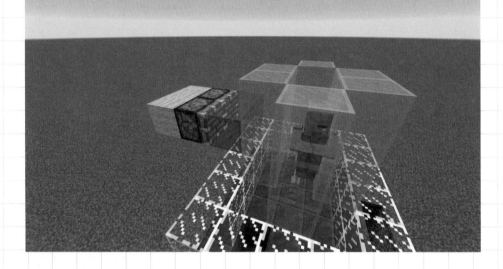

**17.** Add levers above the temporary blocks.

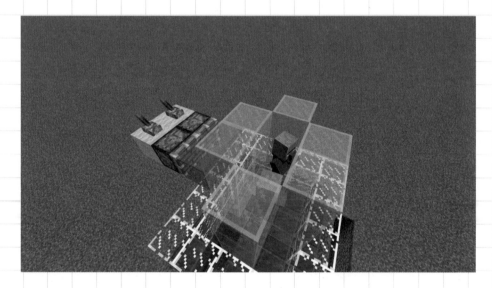

**18.** When the villagers are standing separately in 2 different block spaces, press the levers to extend the pistons and push the glass blocks in.

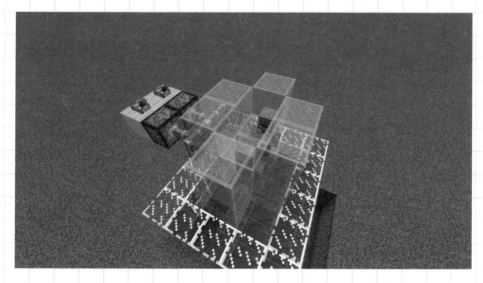

**19.** Remove the pistons, temporary blocks, and levers.

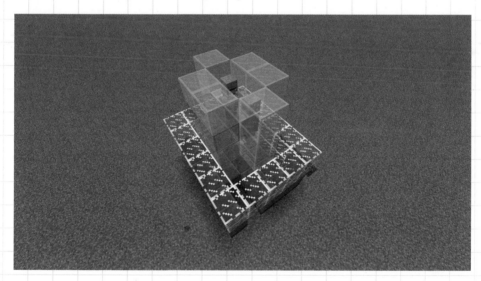

**20.** To finish the village below, push a third villager into the dugout.

**21.** Place lighting inside the dugout to prevent mobs spawning, and add glass blocks above the dugout to prevent mobs jumping in and to make sure the village doors are valid.

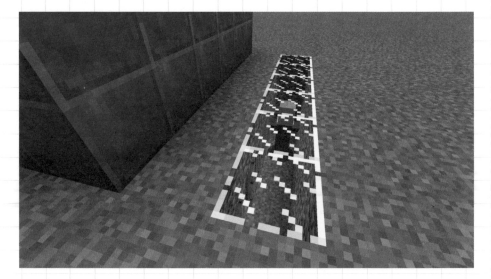

**22.** Place 2 rows of 6 blocks each, connecting to the hole in the farm's base. This will later become a channel for removing baby villagers.

**23.** Inside the enclosure, place a sign over the hole in the base, as shown.

**24.** At the opposite corner, still inside the enclosure, place a bucket of water. The water flow will push villager babies to the hole in the base, and they will drop down.

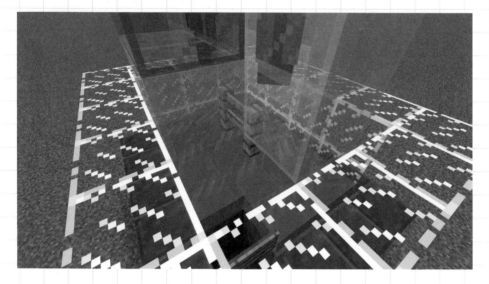

**25.** On top of the enclosure, place 4 blocks to cover up the corner holes in the structure. (You will also want to figure out how you are going to climb up to and get down from the enclosure's top—that is not shown here.)

**26.** Add lighting to the farm to stop mobs from spawning nearby. Add any protective measures to also prevent mobs from wandering in. Zombies can infect villagers through blocks that are joined diagonally, so make sure that they cannot get within a block of the villagers.

**27.** At the bottom of the hole in the base, beneath the sign, place a water block. The water will flow 8 blocks to the end of the channel.

**28.** It is up to you where you want to transport the baby villagers, but you will want them out of range of the existing village so that they don't add to the villager count. You'll also want to protect them with walls, ceilings, and light! Here's a longer water channel. It drops a block every 8 blocks to keep the water flowing and lengthen the channel. At the end is a temporary holding chamber.

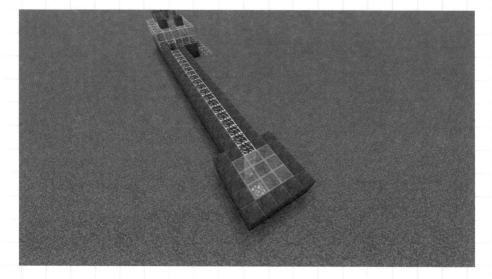

# Corner Danger

ZOMBIES CAN GET AT VILLAGERS THROUGH CORNERS (LEFT). MAKE SURE TO FULLY SURROUND YOUR VILLAGERS WHEN YOU ARE PROTECTING THEM (RIGHT)!

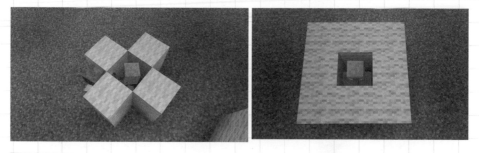

**29.** When you've finished your baby villager collection, transportation, and holding system, it's time to get the villagers breeding. Drop stacks of bread, carrots, or potatoes into the enclosure. It may take 10 minutes or so, but they will start breeding. First, you may see them throwing food at each other. Some time later, hearts will float up from them. After a few rounds of hearts, a baby villager will drop into the stream below, drop into the channel, and away from the enclosure. Congratulations!

# CHAPTER 3
# IRON GOLEM FARM

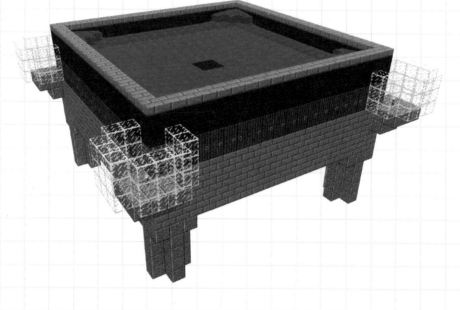

**TIRED OF MINING FOR IRON?** Or need a boatload of cauldrons for some special project? An iron golem farm can bring in over a half-stack of iron every hour, more if you have several going at once! This iron golem farm has been popular in different forms for a long time. It is based on how iron golems spawn within villages. Essentially, you create a village large enough to need an iron golem. You kill each iron golem when it spawns, leaving the village still in need and ready to spawn another golem.

## Iron Golem Details

Iron golems are 2.7 blocks high and 1.4 blocks wide and spawn in villages that have at least 10 villagers and 21 valid houses. They spawn in a 16x16 area, 6 blocks high, centered on the geometric center of the village. One golem can be spawned for every 10 villagers, and the game checks every 6 or so minutes to see if an iron golem can be spawned. Oddly, iron golems can also spawn inside transparent blocks (like glass) as long as they have a solid block to spawn on. Iron golems also cannot be killed by falling or drowning.

## What Makes a Village?

To be recognized by the game as such, a village must have 1 valid house (door) and 1 villager within 16 blocks of the house. A valid house is any door that has at least 1 roof block (a block that blocks sunlight) within 5 blocks behind, and a view to the sky in front. On the skylit side of the door, there must be fewer roof blocks than on the other side, again measured within the 5 blocks directly ahead. This means a valid house can simply be a door by itself with 1 block of dirt behind it.

A village also has a geometric center, which is the average of the coordinates of all the village doors. The village center is subject to changing, however, if villagers recognize "new" doors in the village. The radius of the village is 32 blocks, unless the distance from the center to the farthest door is greater, and then that is the radius. Finally, only doors within a 66-block radius can be counted as within the village. Also, they're only counted once a villager recognizes them. Villagers wander around, and can check doors within 16 blocks of them to see if they are valid and can belong to the village. A village has a maximum population of .35 times the number of houses (doors).

**Note:** You'll want to make sure that your iron golem farm will be about 100 blocks away from any other village. If you want to create several golem farms, make sure that each will be 100 blocks away from any other villages.

## Step by Step

1.  Place a double chest where you will collect the drops from the golems.

2.  Place a hopper facing into the back of the chest. You'll have to shift while placing to do this.

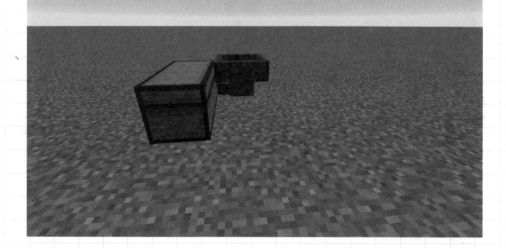

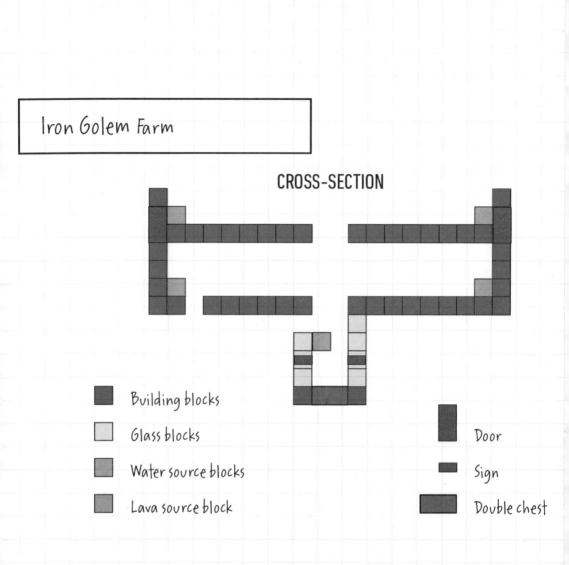

| | Iron Golem Farm |
|---|---|

## CROSS-SECTION

- ■ Building blocks
- □ Glass blocks
- ■ Water source blocks
- ■ Lava source block

- ■ Door
- ■ Sign
- ■ Double chest

## SPACING FOR MULTIPLE FARMS

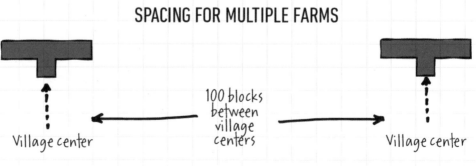

Village center

100 blocks
between
village
centers

Village center

**3.** Place 3 more hoppers as shown, all facing toward the chest. These hoppers will collect the drops from the golems.

**4.** Place a row of building blocks around the collection area, as shown.

**5.** Build up the walls around the collection area another 4 blocks high. Use glass if you can so that you can see when golems fall.

**6.** Now, add another layer of 12 blocks arranged in a square, directly over the collection area's walls. This is the beginning of the first spawning level and is where golems will drop through to the collection and killing area below.

**7.** The spawning level will reach an additional 8 blocks out from the square you built in Step 6. Count out 8 blocks diagonally (or straight, if you prefer) to see where the corners of this level will be, and join the corners. The final square will be 20 blocks by 20 blocks.

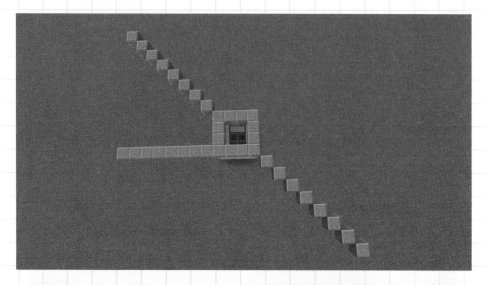

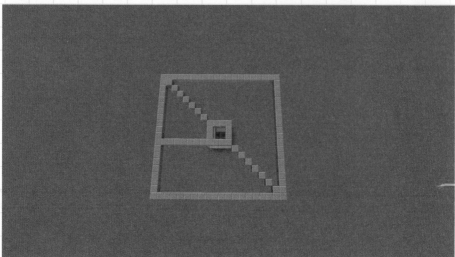

**8.** Fill in the square with solid building blocks.

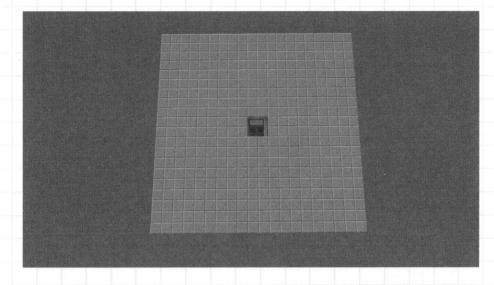

**9.** Add a wall 3 blocks high all around the edge of the platform.

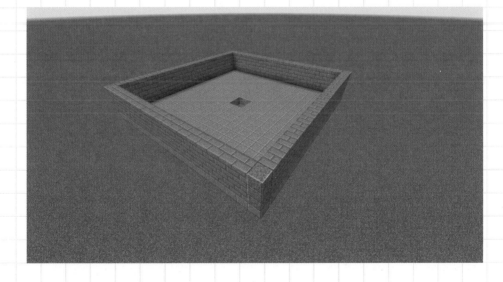

**10.** Raise the 3 adjacent blocks at a corner (the very corner block and the block at each side) another 2 blocks, as shown.

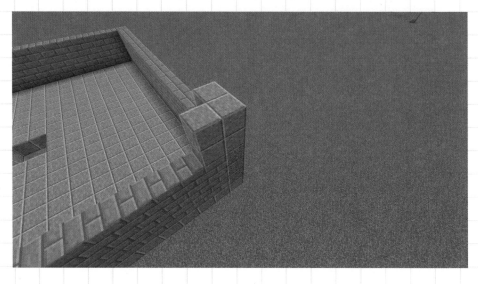

**11.** Do the same for the other 3 corners of the platform.

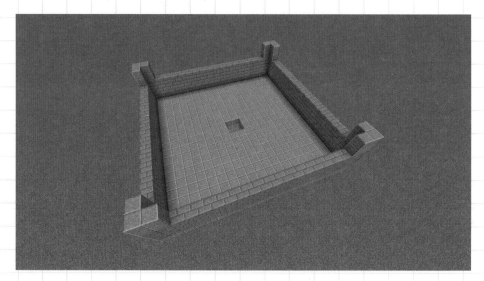

**12.** Place doors along each side of the platform, from 1 corner to the next, as shown.

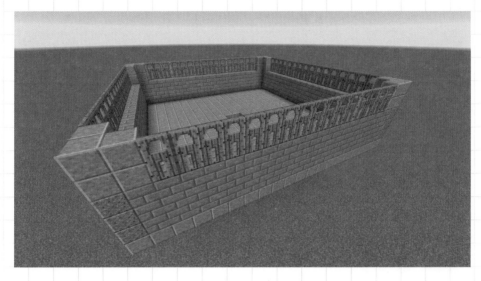

**13.** Inside the platform, in the corner, place 3 temporary blocks. (You'll remove them shortly.) These blocks will help place some of the final water blocks needed.

**14.** Repeat Step 13 at each corner.

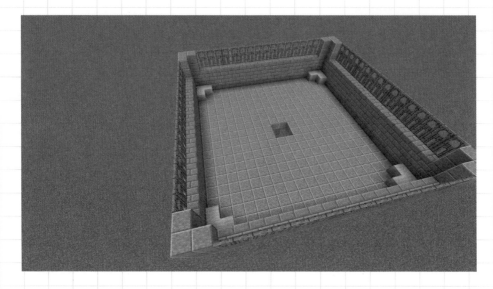

**15.** In between 2 of the temporary corner blocks, place a water source block at every block along the wall. If the platform is the right size, the water will flow to the dropping point and then stop. If this doesn't happen, measure your platform again.

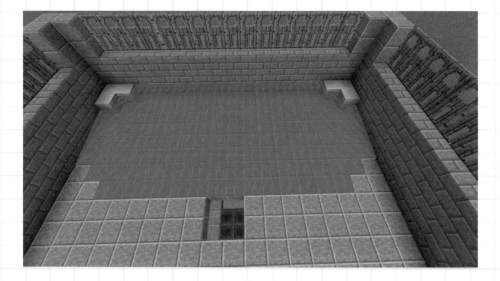

**16.** Repeat Steps 13 and 14 for all sides of the platform.

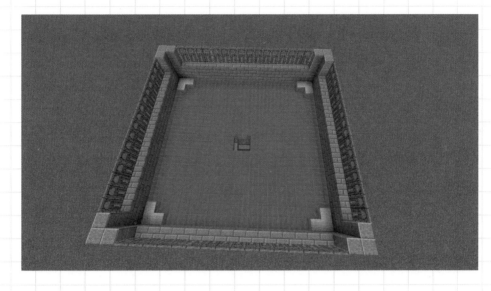

**17.** At 1 corner, place 1 water source block above the temporary block in the very corner. (Don't place any water above the blocks next to this.) This water source will allow the water at the corner to flow to the central drop.

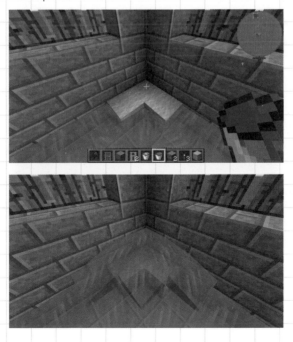

**18.** Now, break the 3 temporary blocks at the corner, so just the water source remains.

**19.** At the 3 other corners of the platform, repeat this process of adding 1 water source and then breaking the temporary blocks.

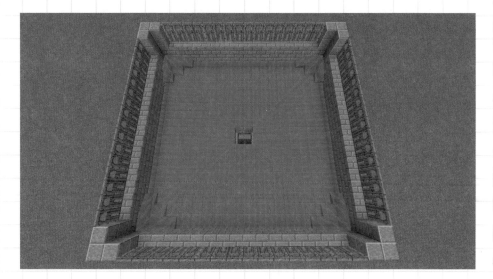

**20.** Now, we'll start building the second spawning area. First, mark the corners of the platform by adding a building block that is 1 block in from the corner walls and at the same height as the top of the doors. (Here, I've used polished granite blocks.)

**21.** Fill in the floor with the corners as guides, as shown.

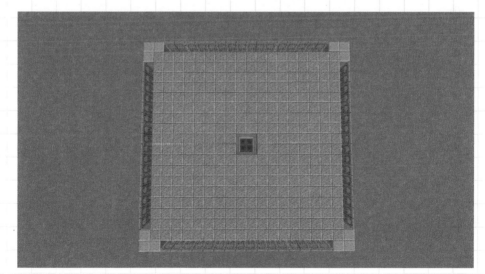

**22.** Place a 2-block-high wall around the platform, right above the doors.

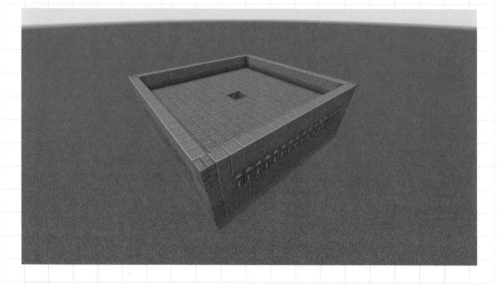

**23.** Add 3 temporary blocks at each corner as shown.

**24.** On each of the 4 walls, place a water source block at each block between the temporary corner blocks.

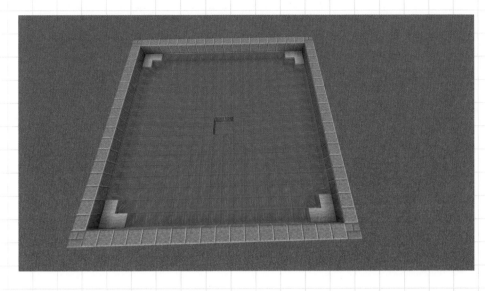

**25.** As you did earlier, place a single water source block at each corner.

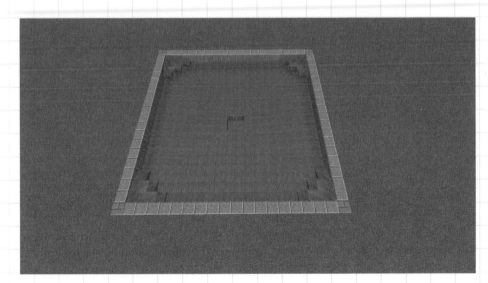

**26.** Break the temporary blocks so that just water is left.

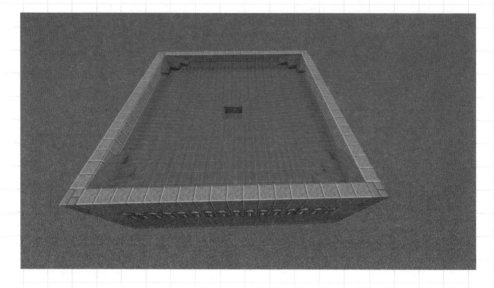

**27.** To prevent mobs spawning on the walls, add a layer of slabs above the walls.

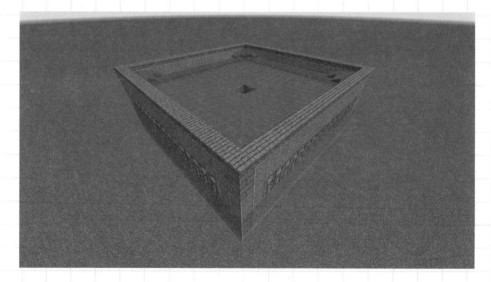

**28.** In the lower level, add a torch on the wall in front of and below every door. This addition will stop mobs spawning inside.

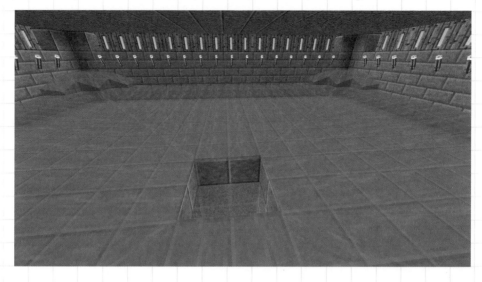

**29.** Back at the collection area, place 2 signs on the left wall above the hoppers and 2 more on the right side. Leave 1 block between the hoppers and the signs.

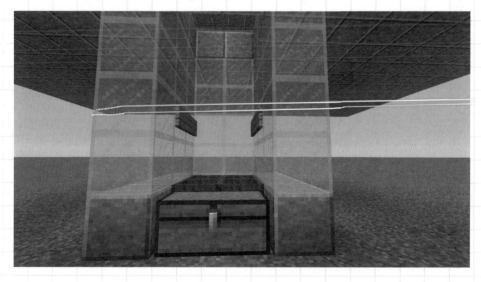

**30.** Add 4 blocks of glass at the front to prevent the lava from flowing forward out of the collection area.

**31.** Now place a single bucket of lava above 1 sign. You can place more above the other signs, but it isn't necessary. The lava will flow to the 3 blocks adjacent to it but no farther.

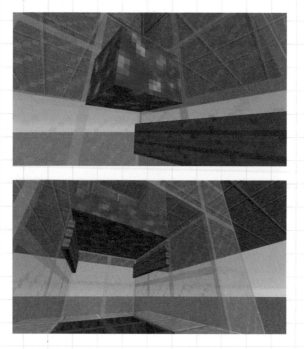

**32.** Close off the collection area with 4 more blocks of glass. When golems spawn above, they will be pushed by the water to the drop and fall through the hole and down to stand on the hoppers. The lava will kill them. But because the lava is at their head level, it won't burn the ingots and poppies the golems will drop when they die.

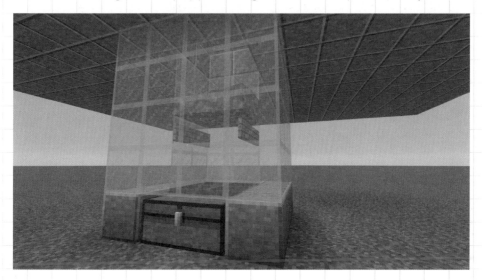

**33.** Now it is time to build the villager enclosures. First, build a squared platform at the corner that extends 3 blocks out from the corner walls, as shown.

**34.** Build walls up 3 blocks high. Glass blocks are best, as they will let you see inside.

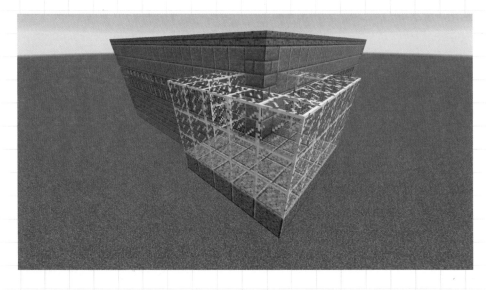

**35.** Repeat Steps 33 and 34 for each corner of the farm.

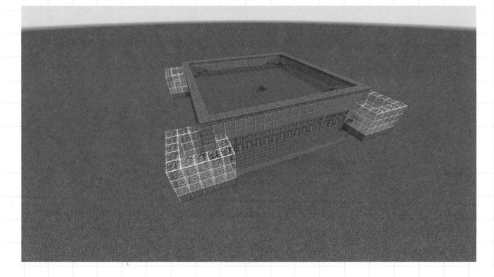

**36.** Here's the tricky bit: You want to have 4 villagers at each corner. The easiest way to do this is to transport 2 villagers by rail to each enclosure, then breed them so that you end up with 4 villagers.

**37.** When you have 4 villagers installed at each corner, add a torch inside each enclosure and cover it with slabs to prevent mobs spawning.

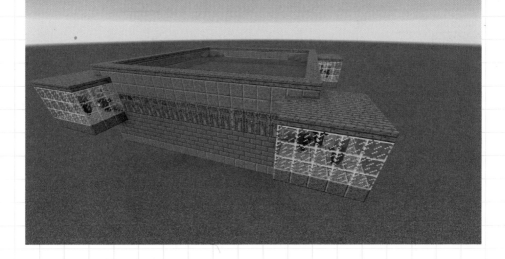

**38.** Your farm is complete. The villagers will need a few minutes to recognize their doors as part of a village. Then the game can recognize all of these doors and villagers as part of a village, one with 12 villagers and 64 doors, in very much need of an iron golem. Within about 6 to 8 minutes, your first iron golem will spawn!

# Need Even More Iron?

ALTHOUGH YOU CAN INCREASE THE NUMBER OF VILLAGERS IN YOUR FARM, THIS STEP WON'T INCREASE YOUR IRON DROPS SIGNIFICANTLY. WHAT WILL INCREASE YOUR IRON SIGNIFICANTLY IS TO HAVE MORE IRON FARM "VILLAGES." THE SIMPLEST WAY TO DO THIS IS TO BUILD A FEW MORE IRON GOLEM FARMS, WHOSE VILLAGE CENTERS ARE 100 BLOCKS AWAY FROM EACH OTHER. BUILD 3 MORE AT GROUND LEVEL, IN A SQUARE. OR YOU COULD EVEN BUILD ABOVE!

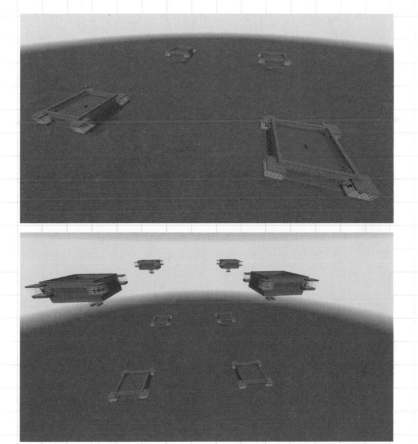

# CHAPTER 4
# CREEPER FARM

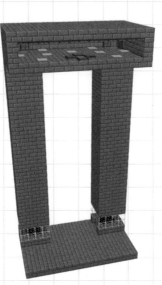

**ONCE YOU HAVE AN ELYTRA,** you will want a steady source of gunpowder to make the rockets that keep you aloft. Happily, the creeper can provide you just that. This creeper farm uses two features of the creeper to make it work:

- Creepers run from cats.

- Creepers are shorter than other 2-block-high mobs, at just 1.7 blocks high. This means you can prevent other mobs from spawning in the farm by keeping the height just enough to fit a creeper.

Like almost all nonspawner mob farms, the drop rate of this creeper farm depends on no other mobs spawning nearby. You can place this creeper in the air, with the base y=124 (or higher) rather than ground level. Or you can light up all the caves and surfaces around within an approximate 130-block radius. It's a large but simple building that is 32 blocks high.

## Step by Step

**1.** Build a base that is 15x15 blocks square.

**2.** On this base, at the corners, will be 4 towers some 25 blocks high that the creepers will drop down. At each corner, mark the location where the towers will be with temporary blocks, as shown.

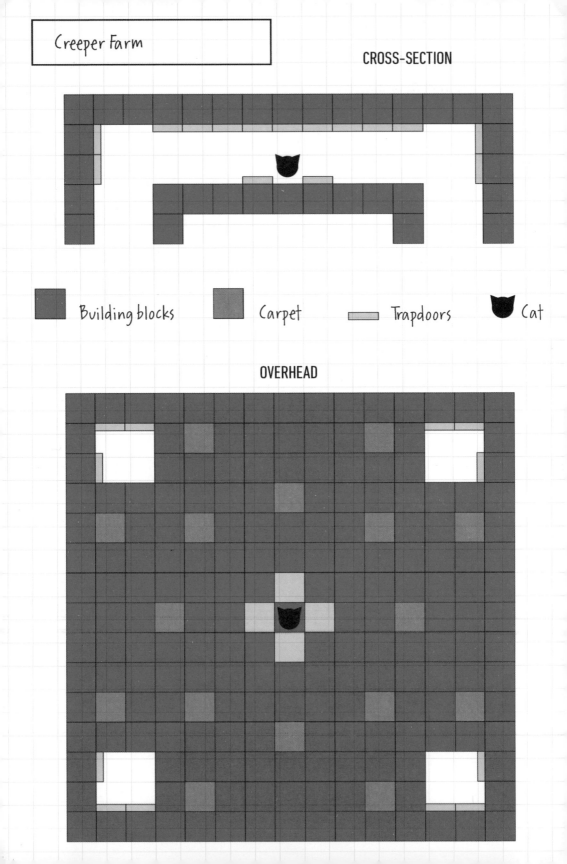

# Creeper Farm

## CROSS-SECTION

**Building blocks**  **Carpet**  **Trapdoors**  **Cat**

## OVERHEAD

**3.** Place a double chest in the center of one of the tower's walls facing the interior of the base.

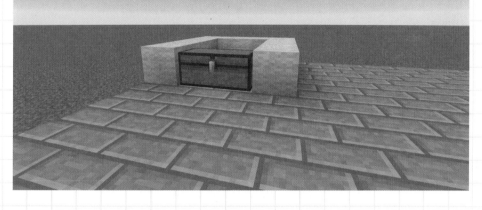

**4.** Repeat Step 3 for the other 3 towers as well.

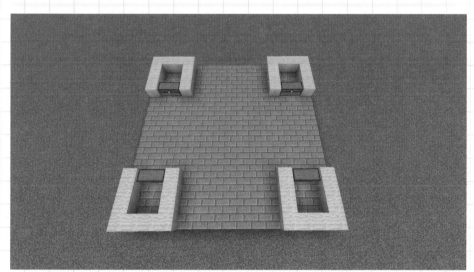

**5.** Place a square of 4 hoppers pointing toward 1 of the double chests, as shown.

**6.** Repeat Step 5 for the other 3 double chests.

**7.** Replace the temporary blocks with building blocks to finish the first layer of the towers.

**8.** Above the first layer of a tower, place 2 rows of glass blocks.

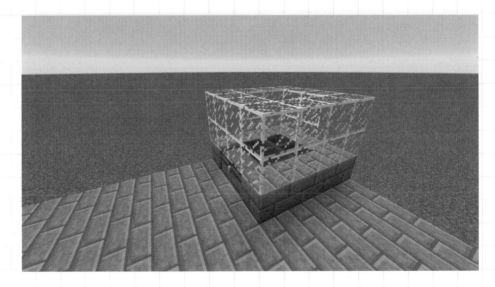

**9.** Repeat Step 8 for the rest of the towers.

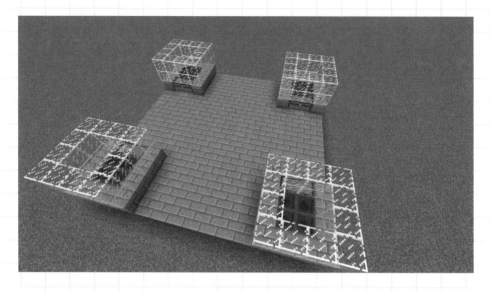

**10.** Above the glass blocks, build each tower up with another 22 layers of blocks.

**11.** When the 4 towers are finished, fill in the area between them to create a square 15x15 platform that has 4 holes in the corners.

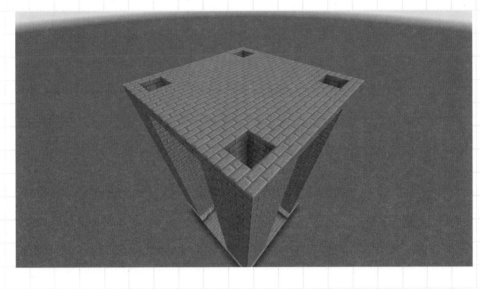

**12.** Build a wall around the platform that is 3 blocks high.

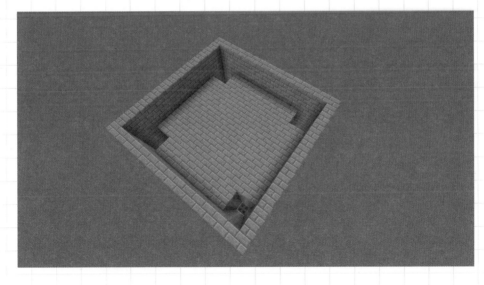

**13.** Find the very center of the platform and place a carpet on it. Then place trapdoors around it, as shown.

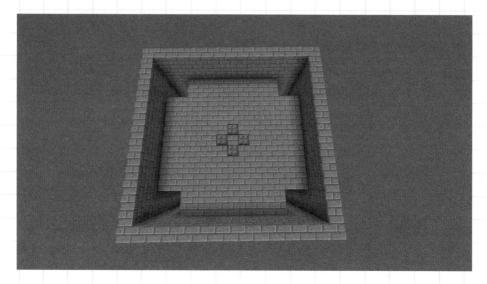

**14.** Now, you need to bring a tamed cat up to sit inside these trapdoors. Your cat should teleport to follow you up to this platform. Once it does, make it sit and then push it to the middle of the trapdoors.

**15.** In one of the corners, above the opening to a tower, place 6 trapdoors as shown on the outer walls.

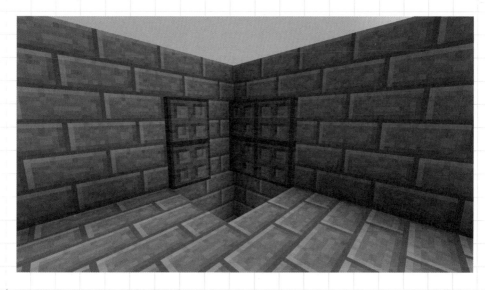

**16.** Repeat Step 15 for the other 3 towers as well.

**17.** Roof in the platform, leaving a 2-block high space within.

**18.** To make the 2-block-high space shorter so that skeletons and zombies will not spawn, place trapdoors on every ceiling block except the blocks above the 4 tower holes.

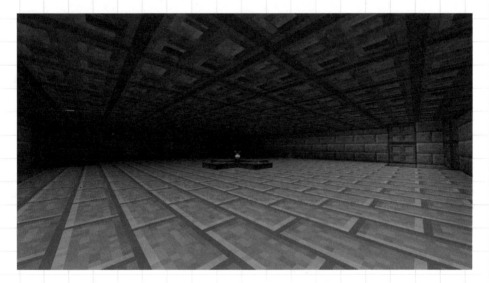

**19.** Place carpets as shown in the cross-section diagram on page 64. These carpets prevent any 3x3 floor spaces for spiders to spawn. Now only creepers can spawn. Hopefully, you have planned your exit! You can loiter around the base between the 4 columns to collect your drops. Don't forget to light up the area and caves to make spawning rates high.

# CHAPTER 5
# AFK FISH FARM

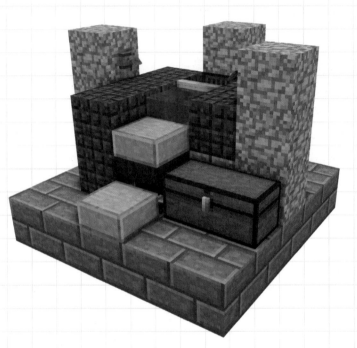

**THIS CONTRAPTION ALLOWS YOU TO STEP** away from the keyboard (AFK) while your game fishes for you until you come back. It is designed so that you can continuously right-click and restart fishing whenever you catch something. And if you fish constantly for 8 or more hours, that adds up to quite a bit of loot!

You can use this farm to really jump-start your game by getting powerful, enchanted books to use on your weapons, tools, and armor. Is it cheating? Some say so, but Minecraft is a sandbox game that's intended for you to play as you like. And, so far, the developers haven't nerfed the ability to make this contraption. Plenty of players use this farm to progress quickly at the start of the game. However, some find it spoils their game by getting too much without effort. You decide!

# Step by Step

1.  Place a building block down with a noteblock on top of it. On top of the noteblock, place another building block to mute the sound of the noteblock.

2.  In front of the topmost block, place another building block.

**3.** In front of this pillar, place an iron door, as shown.

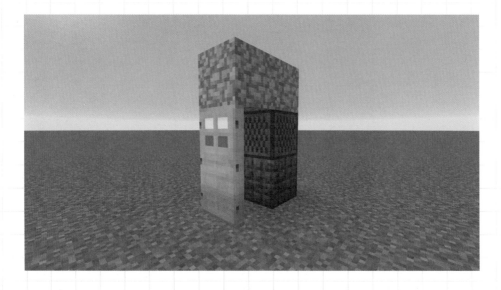

**4.** On 1 side of the iron door, place 2 blocks on the ground, as shown.

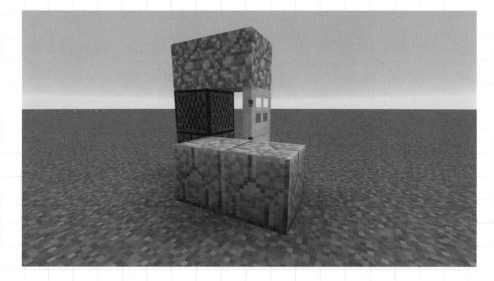

**5.** Add another 2 building blocks on top of these.

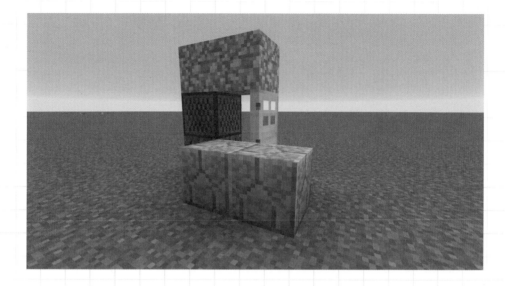

**6.** Do the same for the other side of the iron door. Add 2 blocks on the ground.

**7.** Now add 2 building blocks on top of these.

**8.** Add a 3-block-tall pillar on the left of the wall built in Steps 4 and 5.

**9.** Add another 3-block-tall pillar to the right of the rightmost wall (placed in Steps 6 and 7).

**10.** Place a double chest in front of the right front blocks, as shown.

**11.** Shift-right click with a hopper on the left side of the chest. This will place the hopper so that it is pointed into the chest.

**12.** Shift-right click with a hopper on the back side of the hopper placed in Step 11. Anything dropped into this hopper will now flow directly into the chest.

**13.** Place 1 redstone dust on the block to the right of the iron door, as shown.

**14.** Place a slab on top of the front hopper.

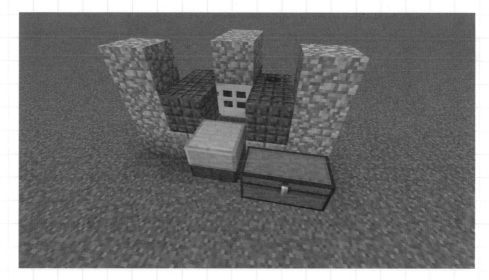

**15.** Place a slab in front of the front hopper, as shown.

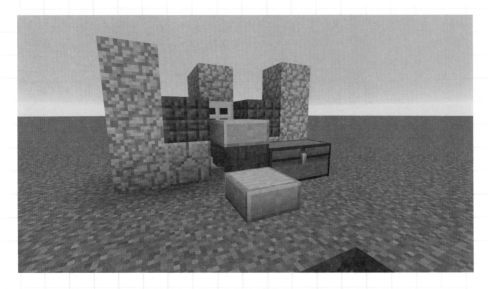

**16.** Place a bucket of water above the back hopper.

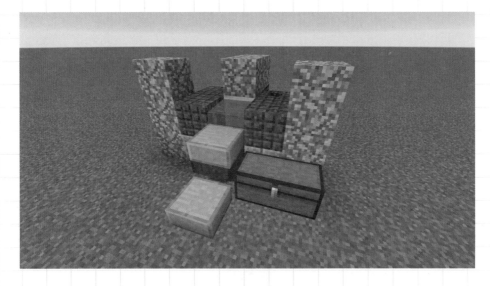

**17.** Add a tripwire hook to the leftmost pillar.

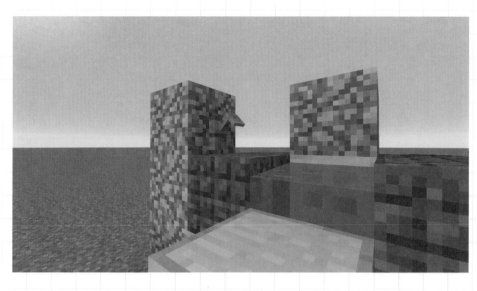

**18.** Add a second tripwire hook to the right pillar.

**19.** Right-click with a piece of string on one of the hooks. This will place the string between the 2 hooks.

**20.** You're all set! To fish, stand on the front slab, and with your fishing rod in hand, point your cursor just below the string, on the top visible edge of the iron door. If you see the hitbox of the string (left), you're aiming too high. Aim lower so that the string's hitbox isn't highlighted (right). Keep pressing down right-click for continuous fishing.

**21.** When you start fishing, the tripwire will still activate, opening the iron door. The iron door will remain open while you are fishing, then close for a moment when a fish is caught and reopen when you begin fishing again. If the door is constantly opening and shutting, you're aiming at the wrong spot.

## How to AFK Fish

To AFK fish, you'll need a way to keep right-clicking while not at your keyboard. There are several ways to do this:

- If a certain glitch is still present, you can press F11 while you right-click to fish. When you release your mouse, the game will assume you are still right-clicking.

- You can keep your right mouse button physically pressed somehow, perhaps with a rubber band or by resting a heavy object on the mouse button.

- Or you can change your controls. When you are ready to go AFK (with your fishing rod in hand and positioned), click Escape, then Options, then Controls to open up the Controls settings. Change Use Item/Place Block to Space. Now change Jump to another key, such as Q. Back in your game, press your spacebar to start fishing. When your cursor is positioned well, you can place a weight on your space bar to keep right-clicking until you come back.

If you are going to be AFK fishing for a long time, you'll want a fishing rod that has Mending on it, so it won't wear down and break. You'll want Lure and Luck of the Sea as well to get the most out of the fishing drop. Don't forget to place more chests as well, connected to each other by hoppers, so you can store the fish and stuff!

If you are playing on a server, make sure that AFK fishing is allowed!

# Fishing Loot

IN ADDITION TO FISH, THE TREASURE YOU CAN GET FROM FISHING INCLUDES BOWS, ENCHANTED BOOKS, FISHING RODS, LILY PADS, NAME TAGS, NAUTILUS SHELLS, AND SADDLES! JUNK YOU CAN GET INCLUDES BONES, BOWLS, INK SACS, LEATHER, LEATHER BOOTS, ROTTEN FLESH, STICKS, STRING, TRIPWIRE HOOKS, AND WATER BOTTLES.

# CHAPTER 6
# WITCH FARM

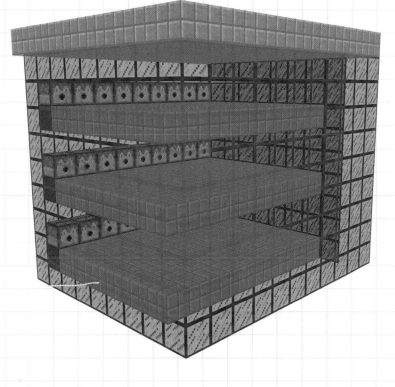

**WITCHES ARE ANOTHER SOURCE BESIDES CREEPERS** to get gunpowder for rockets that will fuel your flying. They'll also supply you with glass bottles, glowstone, redstone, sugar, spider eyes, sticks, water bottles, and the occasional potion! This build uses the spawning area of witch huts.

In this farm, witches spawn on three platforms. Dispensers activate regularly to create a water flow that pushes the witches over the platform edges. From here they are pushed into a contraption that will cause them to die from the entity-cramming rule. The entity-cramming rule in

Minecraft specifies that only 24 entities can occupy the same block space. The 25th entity to enter that space will automatically die. Within the three-dimensional area that the hut takes up, only witches can spawn—you'll never find a skeleton in a witch hut!

As you look for the right witch hut to use, know that the more water that surrounds it, the better. Rarely, witch huts may spawn closely together, or even on top of another witch hut—these are great to use to expand on the witch farm shown in this chapter. Also, before you begin construction, you will need to dispose of any witches inside!

## Step by Step

1.  Begin by marking the border of your first spawning platform. It is 9 blocks by 7 blocks at 1 block above water level. The spawning distance length runs from the edge of the front porch to the edge of the back roof overhang. The width runs between the edges of the overhangs on the sides of the roof.

2. Once the platform is marked, you can remove the witch hut. Choose one of the 9-block-long sides to be the front of the farm, where the witches drop. The other long side will be the back, where the redstone is placed.

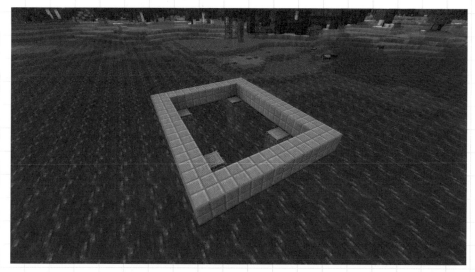

3. If you are surrounded by water, you will ultimately want to remove the water around the front of the farm, and make sure you have a level platform at the back of the farm. You can remove water by dropping sand or gravel. This way, you can easily dig out in the center of the sand as you need to.

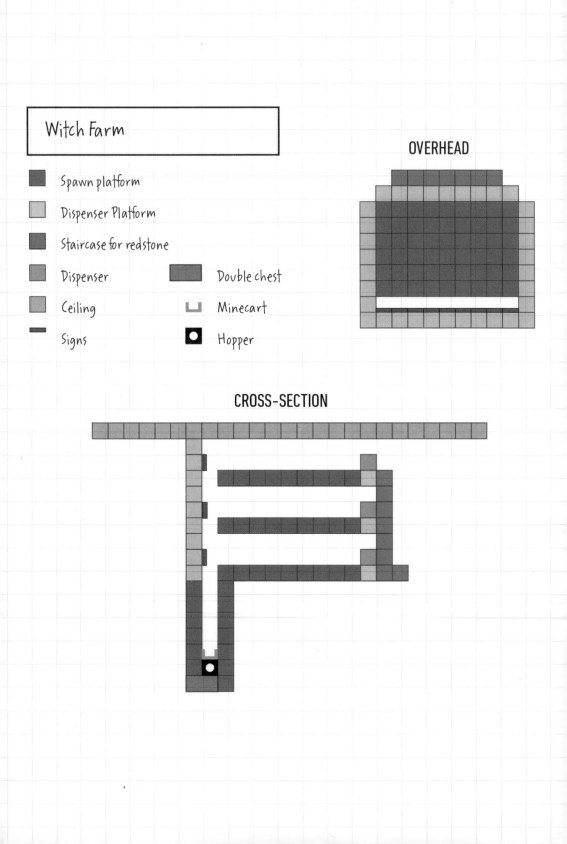

# Witch Farm

- Spawn platform
- Dispenser Platform
- Staircase for redstone
- Dispenser
- Ceiling
- Signs
- Double chest
- Minecart
- Hopper

## OVERHEAD

## CROSS-SECTION

**4.** Because this farm is fully surrounded by water, and to make these instructions and images clearer, I've filled in a much bigger area than necessary around the farm.

**5.** Once you've cleared the area, fill in the bottom platform.

**6.** Build 2 additional, identical platforms above the bottom platform. Each platform is 3 blocks above the lower, leaving 2 blocks of space. Here, I've used temporary yellow wool blocks to show the spacing. It's important to use this exact size of platform, because increasing the size will allow other mobs to spawn in the non-witch-hut areas.

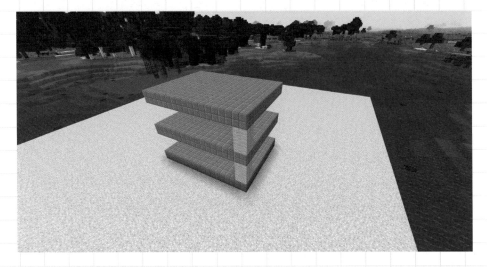

**7.** Create a ceiling over the top platform leaving 2 blocks of space for witches to spawn. The ceiling needs to be large enough so that the light level on each block of each platform is 7 or less. This ceiling extends 9 blocks out from each side of the platforms, bringing the daylight levels down from 15 outside to 5 inside. (The light level drops 1 level per block.)

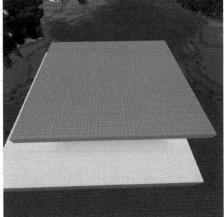

**8.** Build a 7-block-wide, 9-block-tall wall of glass blocks on one of the short sides of the platforms.

**9.** Repeat Step 8 on the opposite side.

**10.** At the back of the farm, add another 9-block-long row of blocks at the back of each platform, as shown. These are used to place the dispensers.

**11.** At the back of a platform, on the row you placed in Step 10, place a row of dispensers facing in, as shown.

**12.** Place a bucket of water in each dispenser. (The bucket can be in any slot of the dispenser's inventory.)

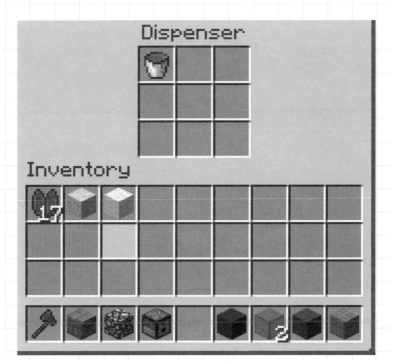

**13.** Repeat Step 12 for the other 2 platforms: Add rows of dispensers each with a water bucket inside.

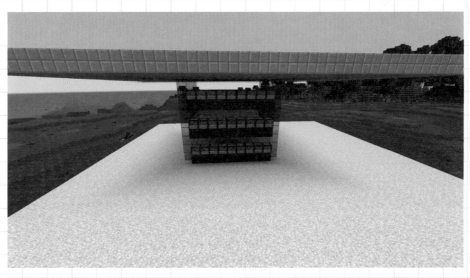

**14.** At the front of the farm, build an 11-block-wide, 9-block-tall wall of glass blocks, 2 blocks out from the front edge of the platforms (leaving 2 blocks of space).

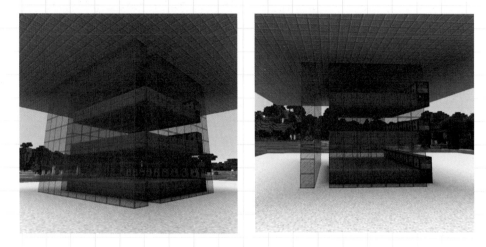

**15.** Across from one of the platforms on the new wall, place a row of 9 signs as shown. These signs will prevent the water flow from the dispenser from flowing over the edge.

**16.** Repeat Step 15 for the other 2 platforms.

**17.** Now, we'll add the redstone that will activate the dispensers. First, place redstone on top of all of the dispensers.

**18.** Use any building block to create an 8-block-wide by 10-block-long floor that the redstone circuits will be on. Locate the floor as shown, up against the bottom platform, with its top right corner placed 3 blocks in from the side of the platform.

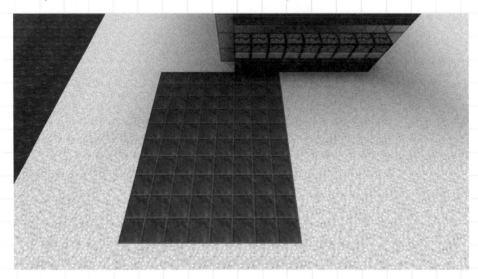

**19.** Use 7 blocks to build a staircase from ground level to just below the top row of dispensers as shown. This staircase will carry the redstone signal from the source to each dispenser.

**20.** Now to the redstone circuits: First, we will build an Etho hopper clock that will time when the water is placed to flush the witches out from the platforms. Start by placing a temporary block 4 blocks in from the outer edge of the floor on the left side, as shown.

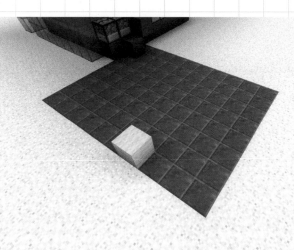

**21.** On the side nearer the farm, place a hopper pointing into the temporary block.

**22.** Break the temporary block. In its place, put a hopper pointed into the first hopper.

**23.** Place a comparator facing out from the back of 1 hopper.

**24.** Place a second comparator facing out from the back of the other hopper.

**25.** Add a block on each side for the comparators to face into, as shown.

**26.** Add 2 redstone dust, each beside 1 of the 2 blocks just placed.

**27.** Place a sticky piston with its back to 1 of the redstone dust, as shown.

**28.** Place a second sticky piston with its back to the other redstone dust and facing the first sticky piston.

**29.** Place 2 temporary blocks between the 2 pistons. This is where we will place a redstone block that will be pushed from 1 piston to the other. The redstone block will be the source of the redstone power that will turn on and off the waterworks.

**30.** We will be taking the signal from where the left temporary block is. In front of this block, place an observer block, with its face pointing in to the temporary block and output side facing outward.

**31.** We're going to run the future signal from the observer block to the stairs. First, place a repeater facing in to the bottom step, as shown. This will make sure the signal is strong enough to reach all the dispensers.

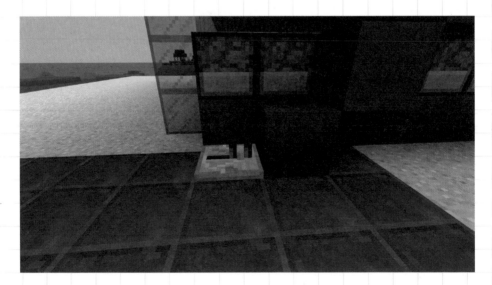

**32.** Now use 8 redstone dust to run a line between the output side of the observer block to the back of the repeater.

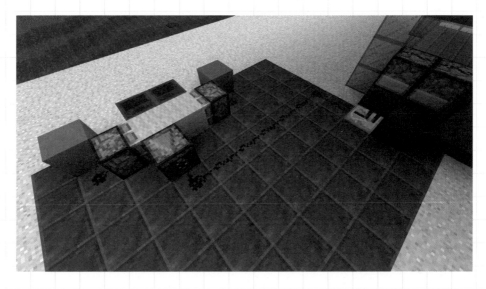

**33.** Place a line of redstone dust between the front of the repeater, up the stairs, and to the top block of the stairs. This finishes the power line that will place the water to flush out the witches.

**34.** Now we will need a second signal that will activate the dispensers a second time so that they will pick up the water they placed. We need to give enough time for the water to move all witches off the platform. We'll use repeaters to delay the signal. First, add a block to the staircase, as shown. This is where the second signal will connect to the dispensers.

**35.** Place a redstone dust on top of the block you just added.

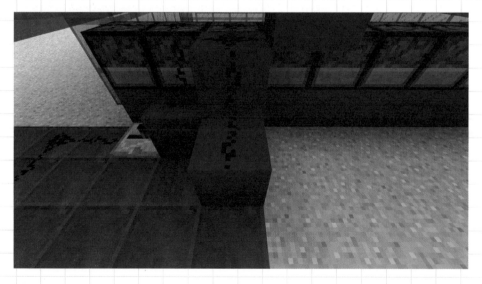

**36.** Place a repeater facing into the block.

**37.** Place 6 more repeaters in a line, also facing toward the stairs.

**38.** Place a second line of 5 repeaters, facing away from the stairs, next to the first line, as shown.

**39.** Place a third line of just 2 repeaters, facing toward the farm, as shown.

**40.** Place 2 redstone dust to link the last line of repeaters with the middle line.

**41.** Place 2 more redstone dust to link the middle line of repeaters with the line of repeaters leading to the stairs.

**42.** Click each repeater 3 times to set it to the longest delay. When this is done, the 2 tiny redstone lamps on the repeater will be at opposite ends of the repeater's base.

**43.** Place 1 last repeater leading away from the redstone dust in front of the observer block.

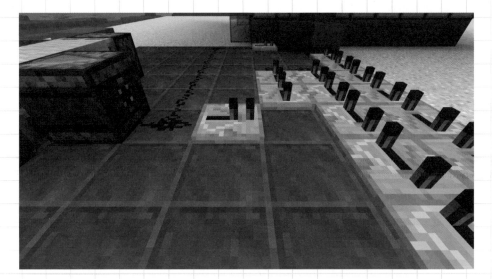

**44.** Add 1 redstone dust to connect this last repeater to the chain of repeaters going to the stairs.

**45.** Remove the temporary blocks between the pistons. This will alert the observer block, and the 2 signals—one to start the water and the second to remove it—will be sent. Place a redstone block on the right block between the hoppers.

**46.** To start the clock, place 64 blocks of any type, such as cobblestone, into 1 of the hoppers. The hoppers will start transferring the blocks to each other, moving the redstone block between them. When the observer block senses the update in front of it, it will send a signal out its back. The signal is split into two, one that activates the dispensers to place water and the second to pick the water back up again.

**47.** Now it is time to tackle the collection and killing area. First, dig a trench that is 3 blocks deep between the front of the platforms and the glass wall with signs on it. The trench should run from the edge of 1 side of the platforms to the glass wall on the other, 10 blocks long in total, as shown.

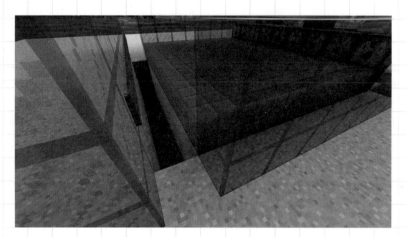

**48.** Dig out a workspace that will hold the killing area and chest storage: I've dug out an area. You will want to dig a space that is 4 blocks deeper than the trench.

**49.** Place a water source at the opposite end of the trench. This will show how far the witches will be pushed.

**50.** Enclose the opposite end of the trench with glass blocks, as shown.

**51.** At the place where the trench's water stream ends, dig 4 blocks down.

**52.** At the bottom of this hole, place a double chest.

**53.** Add a hopper facing down into the chest.

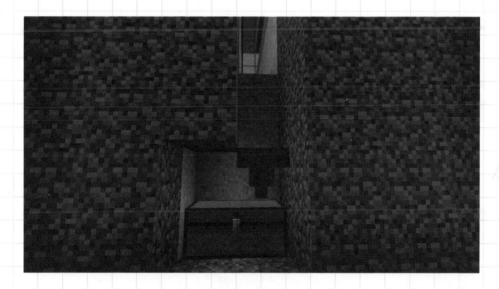

**54.** Place a single rail on top of the hopper.

**55.** Place a minecart with hopper on top of the hopper. With your cursor highlighting the rail, place 23 more minecarts. These will join invisibly to the minecart with hopper. (These 24 minecarts are entities, and when a single witch drops into the space, they will die.)

**56.** Once this is complete, click very carefully on the rail to break and remove it. The carts will move down slightly to rest on the hopper.

**57.** Enclose the minecarts and the drop above the carts with glass.

**58.** Fill in the space between the glass block walls above the drop with more glass blocks. Make sure the spawning area is enclosed, and protect your redstone area from accidents and creepers. Place slabs around the farm to prevent mobs from spawning.

**59.** To get really good rates for drops, you will have to light up all the caves and surfaces in the area, within approximately 150 blocks. It is a chore, but it will be well worth it. It is important to try to light up all the caves, because even 5% of the caves left dark will hurt your spawning rate at the witch farm. (Mobs won't spawn on water, so that helps!)

# CHAPTER 7
# BLAZE FARM

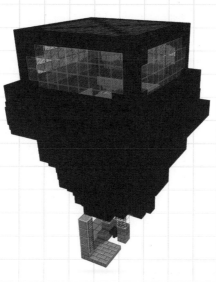

**IF YOU ARE KEEN ON MAKING** lots of potions, or if you'd like to have a great way to up your XP, you'll want to go a step further and make your own Blaze farm. This farm collects spawning blazes into an increasingly smaller funnel. They are pushed down into a single block where you can kill them to reap a bounty of rods and XP.

Blazes can spawn at higher light levels, so the best way to prevent them from spawning is to block in their spawn area completely. Since you will be digging down below the spawner, make sure that you'll be protected from falling into lava. Guard against ghast fireballs with temporary cobblestone walls and shelters, and add single rows of blocks in corridors to prevent wither skeletons from getting closer. You will also want enchanted armor and weapons to help protect against Blaze fireballs (Fire/Projectile damage) and Ghast fireballs (Explosion/Projectile damage). An Efficiency enchanted pick to help you break blocks faster is a help, and potions for protection and healing are a huge aid.

## Step by Step

1. To prevent blazes from spawning from the spawner, fill in the spawn area with blocks that are easy to break. Fill in a 9x9x5 area, centered vertically and horizontally on the spawner.

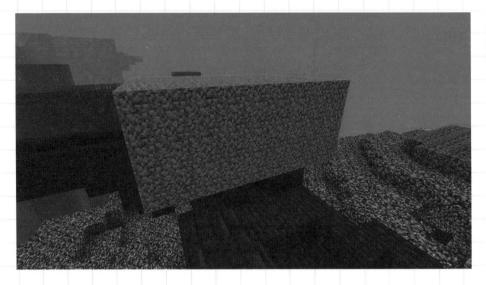

*Now we'll begin creating the funnel, with layers of pistons that will push blazes toward the center as they fall. (We can't use water, because water doesn't work in the Nether!) The images for these next steps will usually only show the blocks that must be placed. However, in order to place these blocks shown, you will likely need to place some temporary blocks first, especially to help with positioning the pistons. Dirt is a good option, as it is easy to break.*

*To make illustrating the build clearer, let's move to a creative Overworld!*

**2.** On one side of the spawn area, 1 block down and 3 blocks out (leaving a 2-block space), place a row of 9 building blocks. (I've used polished andesite.) These blocks will be used to help place pistons and as a guard against ghast fireballs. I've used temporary yellow wool blocks just to show the spacing here.

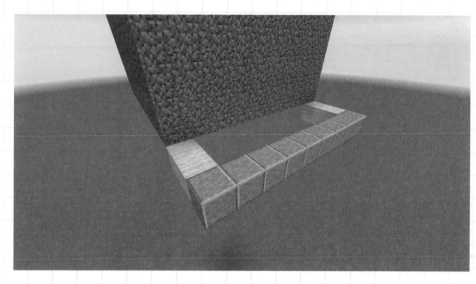

**3.** Repeat Step 2 on the opposite wall of the dirt cuboid.

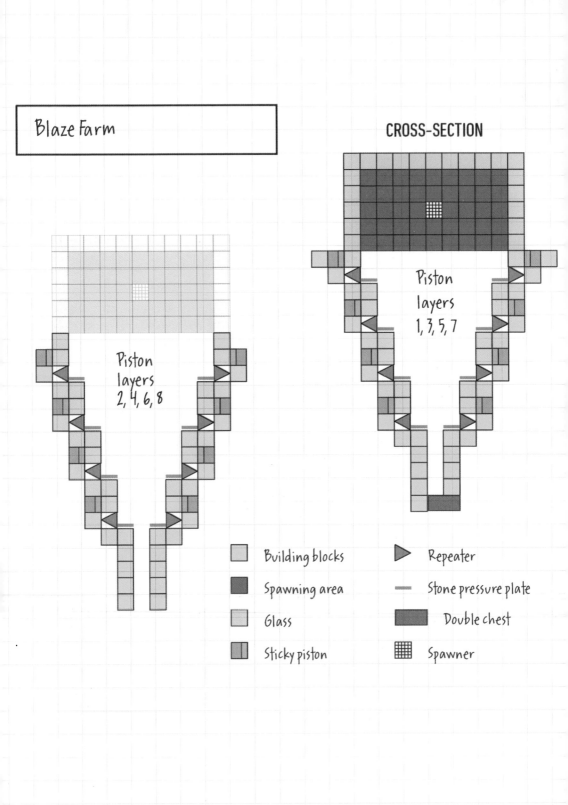

Blaze Farm

CROSS-SECTION

Piston layers 2, 4, 6, 8

Piston layers 1, 3, 5, 7

Building blocks

Spawning area

Glass

Sticky piston

Repeater

Stone pressure plate

Double chest

Spawner

**4.** Place 2 rows of 9 sticky pistons each (18 total) against the 2 building block rows.

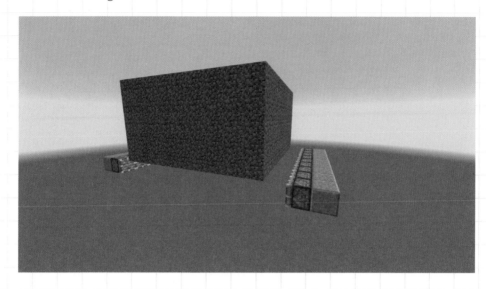

**5.** Now place 2 rows of 9 solid blocks in front of the piston rows. (I've used polished granite.) These blocks are used to push the blazes into the center.

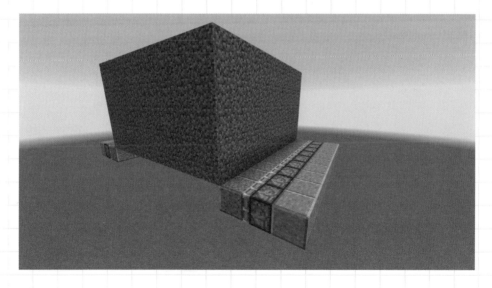

**6.** Underneath each row of pistons, place a row of solid blocks. (I've used stone bricks.)

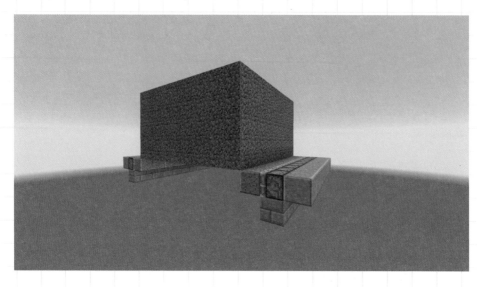

**7.** Just 1 block below and 1 block in from the row placed in Step 6, add a 2-block-wide row of 9 solid blocks, as shown.

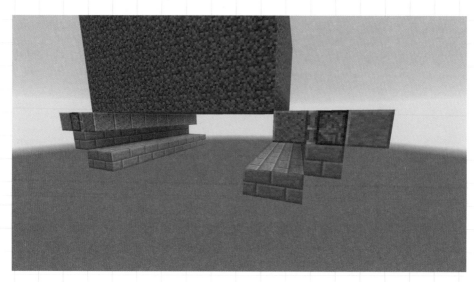

**8.** Place a row of 9 repeaters, facing outward, toward the row of blocks placed in Step 6. In front of these, place a row of stone pressure plates. Do this on both sides. This is the first layer of pistons that will push blazes toward the center. If a blaze lands on one of these pressure plates, a signal will carry through the repeater and into the block it faces. The piston above will activate and extend, and the block it pushes will force the blaze 1 block in to the center. Then the piston and its block will move back to their original position.

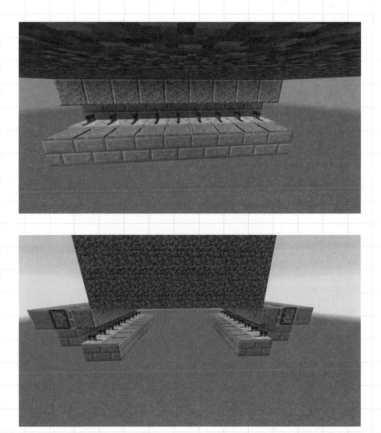

*To complete the next level of the funnel, we'll repeat Steps 2 through 8, but work on the other 2 sides of the spawn area. We'll also move 1 block down and 1 block in from either corner. Along with the following steps, you can use the diagram on page 122 to help place blocks.*

**9.** Move to one of the sides between the existing rows of pistons. At 1 block down and 3 blocks out from the dirt cuboid (leaving a 2-block space), and 1 block in from each corner, place a row of 7 building blocks. (I've used polished andesite again.) Temporary yellow wool blocks show the spacing. Do this on the opposite side as well.

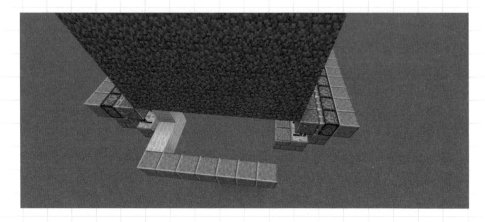

**10.** In front of each of the 2 new rows of building blocks, place a row of 7 sticky pistons and a row of 7 solid blocks in front of the pistons.

**11.** Below the 2 new rows of pistons, place a row of building blocks.

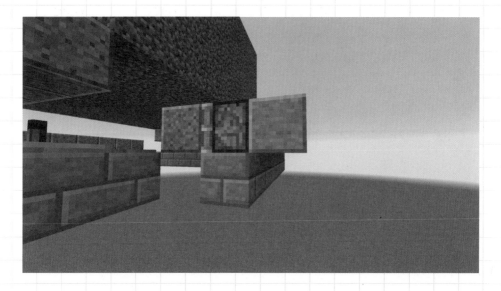

**12.** Below these, and a block in, place a 2-wide row of building blocks.

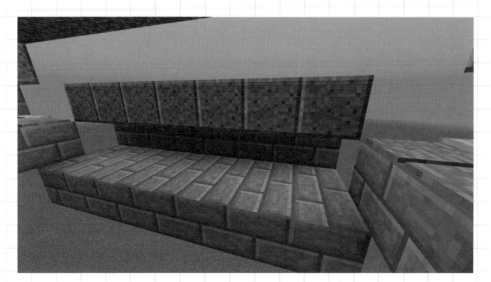

**13.** On the blocks placed in Step 12, place a row of 7 repeaters and a row of 7 stone pressure plates. Do this on both sides.

**14.** Now we turn to the other pair of opposite walls. We'll place another 2 rows of the pushing mechanism, 1 row down but still 7 blocks wide. First, place a row of 7 pistons right below the row of solid blocks placed in Step 6. Repeat on the opposite side.

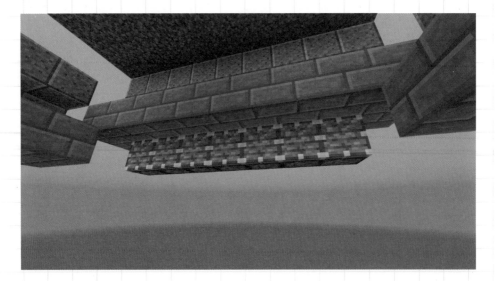

**15.** In front of the pistons, place a row of 7 solid blocks. Do this on the opposite side, as well.

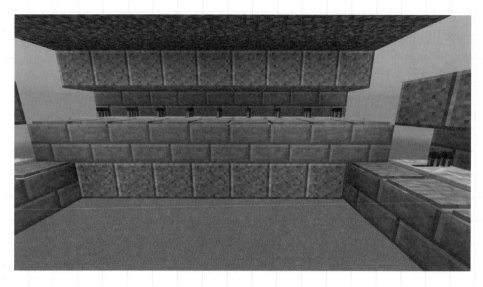

**16.** On both sides, directly below the pistons, place another row of 7 blocks, and in front of these and down 1 block, place the 2-wide row of blocks that will hold the 7 repeaters and 7 pressure plates.

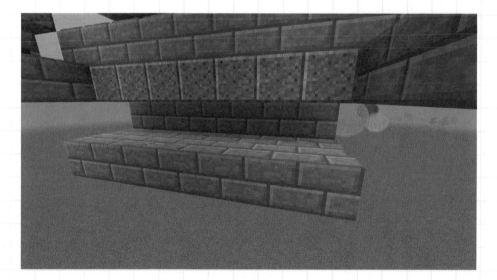

**17.** Add the row of 7 repeaters and 7 pressure plates on top of the 2-wide platforms built in Step 16. Do this on the opposite side as well.

*The next steps are basically exactly the same as Steps 9 through 17, except that the length of the rows is now 5.*

**18.** Place a row of 5 pistons below the row of building blocks that the repeaters are on, which were built in Step 12. Do this on the opposite side as well.

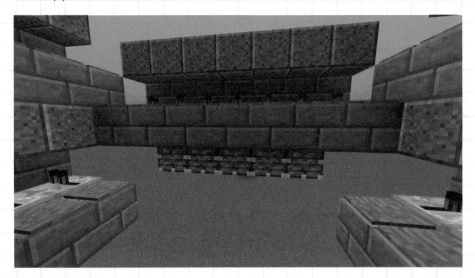

**19.** Place 5 building blocks (I've used granite) in front of the pistons on each side.

**20.** Below the pistons, place a row of building blocks (stone bricks, here). Do this on both sides.

**21.** In front of these and 1 block down, place the 2-wide row of building blocks that the repeaters and pressure plates go on. Again, do this on both sides.

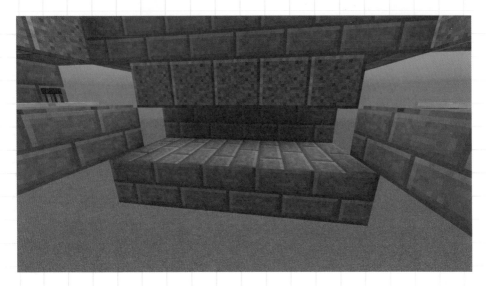

**22.** On each side, place the 5 repeaters and 5 pressure plates on the 2-wide platform, as shown.

**23.** Moving to the second pair of opposite sides, place 5 pistons below the row built in Step 16. Make sure to perform these steps on the opposite wall as well.

**24.** Place building blocks in front of the pistons (granite, here).

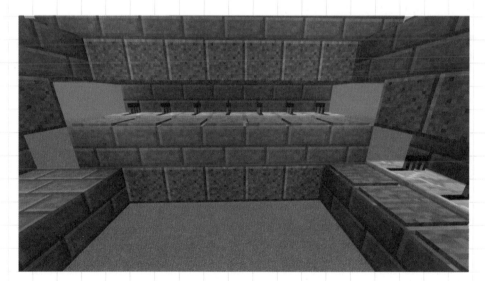

**25.** Below the pistons, place a row of building blocks (stone bricks, here).

**26.** In front of and down 1 from the row built in Step 25, add the 2-wide row that will hold the 5 repeaters and 5 pressure plates.

**27.** Add the 5 repeaters and 5 pressure plates.

*We're now ready to reduce the sides of the funnels to 3 pistons long. This final set of 4 walls each with 3 pistons will force the blazes into the very center single block of space. Again, remember to perform these steps on the opposite walls as well.*

**28.** Below the blocks placed to hold repeaters in Step 22, add a row of 3 pistons.

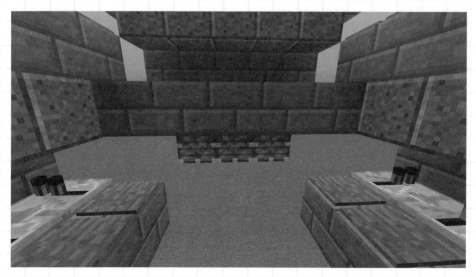

**29.** In front of the 3 pistons, place a row of 3 solid blocks (here, polished granite).

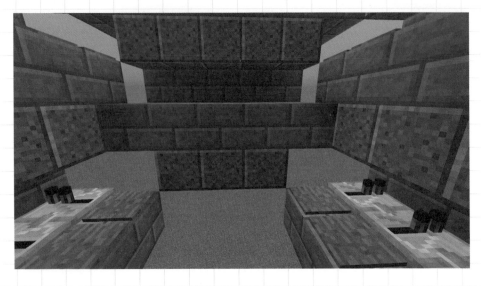

**30.** Below the pistons, add another row of building blocks.

**31.** In front of, and down 1 block from the row in Step 30, add the 2-side platform that will hold the 3 repeaters and 3 pressure plates.

**32.** Place the 3 repeaters and 3 pressure plates on the platform.

**33.** Repeat Steps 28 through 32 on the second pair of opposite walls.

Now, we'll just need 2 final pistons, on opposite sides of the funnel, to push the blazes into a single block space.

**34.** Below the blocks holding the repeaters that you built in Step 26, add a single piston on each wall.

**35.** Place a block in front of the piston.

**36.** Place a block beneath the piston.

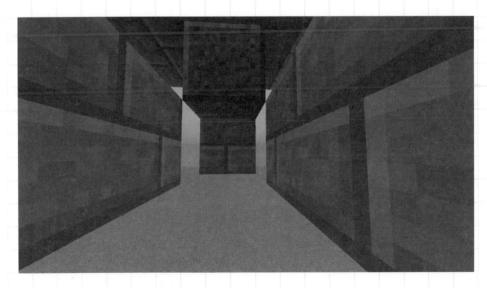

**37.** Place a 2-wide platform (1 long), in front of and 1 down from the block placed in Step 36.

**38.** Add a repeater and pressure plate above the platform as shown.

**39.** Add 2 building blocks to the bottom of the 2 sides of the funnel that are higher than the other 2, as shown.

**40.** Below the bottom 4 blocks of the funnel, add another 4 glass blocks.

**41.** Add another 4 blocks of glass below these.

**42.** Below each of the back and 2 side glass blocks, add 2 stone blocks. Once enclosed, this will be the killing area.

**43.** In front of the killing area, add a double chest, as shown.

**44.** Place a hopper behind the double chest and pointing into the chest. This will collect the blaze rods.

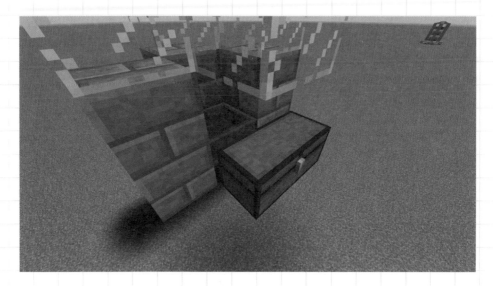

**45.** Add a stone block to the side of the double chest.

**46.** In front of the chest, add a 3x3 platform of bottom slabs.

**47.** At one of the front corners of the 3x3 platform, add a top slab.

**48.** On top of the doubled slab, add 4 building blocks. When you stand at the top of this pillar, you will be within range of the blaze spawner and blazes will spawn and be funneled down to the killing area. (They'll stop spawning when you are below this pillar's top.)

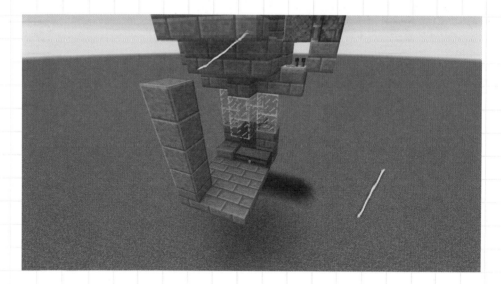

**49.** Add a way to get down quickly to the killing area from the pillar.

**50.** Almost complete! Now, all you have to do is enclose the dirt cuboid covering the spawn area and the blaze farm funnel so that ghast balls can't get in or hit the pistons. Plan out an escape from the interior before you get rid of the dirt cuboid! Here, I've used red nether brick and orange glass to finish off the blaze farm. You will also want to add protective building for yourself while you're at the farm. You can add bottom slabs above blocks to prevent spawnage of unwanted mobs.